EUDIST PRAYERBOOK SERIES: VOLUME 4

34 Flames of Divine Love

ELEVATIONS OF THE HEART TOWARD GOD
by St. John Eudes

Compiled by *Heart of Home* from:
The Life And The Kingdom Of Jesus in Christian Souls: A Treatise On Christian Perfection For Use By Clergy Or Laity

Translated from the French
by Thomas Merton
Originally published 1946
(New York: P. J. Kenedy & Sons)

Layout by Deanna Heitschmidt

Cover image: a 40 ton marble statue of St. John Eudes in St. Peter's Basilica. Carved in 1932 by Silvio Silva, this is one of 39 large statues around the Basilica's nave and transepts honoring the founders of great religious orders.

ISBN: 978-0-9979114-3-5

Copyright ©2018, by
The Eudists – Congregation of Jesus and Mary, US Region

All Rights Reserved.

Published by

PO Box 3619
Vista, CA 92085-3619
eudistsusa.org

No part of this publication may be reproduced in any form or by any means, including scanning, photocopying, or otherwise without prior written permission of the copyright holder: The Eudists – Congregation of Jesus and Mary, US Region.

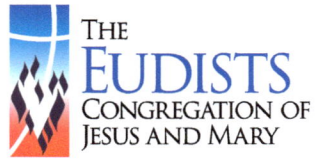

Table of Contents

Preface 1
1. "You are all love, infinitely lovable 3
2. "Alas, this poor heart of mine 3
3. "Jesus, worthy of all desire 3
4. "Hearken to the cry of my heart 4
5.* "Crown of desire 4
6. "Who would not wish to love you? 4
7. "Oh king of my heart 4
8. "You are all love, and all love for me 5
9. "I surrender entirely to your might 5
10. "Pure flame of love 5
11. "My sweet love 6
12. "Oh king of my love 8
13. "Life of my life, soul of my soul 8
14. "Sole object of my heart 8
15. "You alone are worthy of love 8
16. "Only love of my heart 8
17. "Detach me from myself, draw me to you 9
18. "How lovable, yet so little loved 9
19. "Eternal Son of the Eternal Father 9
20. "Oh eternal love 9
21. "Everlasting beauty 10
22. "You have bought with your blood 10
23. "You are everywhere and in all things 11
24. "An infinite love would be necessary 11

---

* Elevation #5 was later used by Venerable Amelie Fristel (foundress of the Congregation of the Holy Hearts of Jesus and Mary) as her daily morning offering.

25. "If I had every single heart 11

26. "The abyss of my nothingness 12

27. "The Father loves us as He loves you 12

28. "You are purity itself 13

29. "Dearest friend of my heart 14

30. "When shall I love you purely? 14

31. "You employ all your powers to testify 15

32. "I love you, I love you, Lord Jesus 17

33. "I desire further, oh my Jesus 17

34. "When will the time come? 18

Acts of Love for Jesus, Prisoner in the
Sacred Womb of His Most Blessed Mother 20

Acts of Love in Honor of the Birth
and Holy Childhood of Jesus 21

Conclusion 22

Addenda 23

    A Note on the Translators 24

    About St. John Eudes 26

    About the Eudist Family 30

Introduction

Of all the duties and functions of a truly Christian soul, the most noble, most holy, most elevated that God asks of you before all others, is to exercise yourself in divine love. For this reason you must make a point of affirming to Jesus Christ our Lord, in all your pious practices and other actions, that you desire to perform them, not for fear of hell, nor for the reward of heaven, nor for the merit attached, nor for your own satisfaction and consolation, but only for the love of God Himself, for His satisfaction, His glory and His pure love.

So, too, you ought frequently to exercise yourself by contemplation and acts of this divine love.

I have already indicated many such acts in this book *[The Life and Kingdom of Jesus in the Christian's Soul]*. But in addition, here are thirty-four more, in honor of the thirty four years of Our Lord's life on earth, a life that was all love. Added to these are one or two others which may be used at any time, but are chiefly intended for the monthly day of recollection or any other day in the month set aside expressly for your conscientious application to this divine contemplation, which is the greatest, the holiest, and most noble occupation of the angels and saints, and of God Himself, in which He always has been, is now, and ever shall be engaged throughout all the infinite extent of eternity.

    John Eudes
    Missionary Priest
    Caen, France, 1636

Thirty-Four Acts of Love of Jesus Christ in Honor of the Thirty-Four Years of His Life on Earth

1. Oh Jesus, my Savior, You are all love, infinitely lovable and infinitely worthy of love. Oh my God, I need no other knowledge but this. What concern have I with so many studies and ideas and considerations? It suffices me to know that my Jesus is all lovable, and that there is nothing in Him that is not worthy of being loved beyond measure. Let my mind then he satisfied with this knowledge; but may the hunger of my heart to love Him who can never be loved enough, never be sated.

2. Alas! My Savior, I know that this poor, insignificant, imperfect heart of mine is not worthy to love You. But You are exceedingly worthy to be loved, and You created this poor heart only that it might love You. You command it to love You under pain of death, eternal death. God of my heart, You have no need to command. To love You is what I want, what I desire, what my heart sighs after. Yes, my Jesus, I no longer want any other desire. Farewell all other thoughts, all other inclinations, all other wishes. I wish to have but one overwhelming purpose here on earth; I desire nothing, only to love Jesus, who is the love and delight of heaven and earth. Ah, Jesus! Ah, My Dear Jesus! What do I desire on earth? Nothing, oh my all, but only to love You.

3. Oh Jesus, worthy of all desire, indeed I long to love You, not only with all the power of my too feeble will, but to the full extent and with all the might of Your divine will, which is mine since You have given me all. Add to that the will of all men and angels. They also are mine, since in giving Yourself to me You have given me everything. Oh sweetest Lord, would that I were entirely transformed into desires, aching, yearning, and longing to love You ever more and more!

4. Oh desire of my soul, grant me the favor I implore; hearken to the cry of my heart. You know, Lord, what I ask of You; my heart has so often told You. I ask nothing but the perfection of Your holy love. I desire only to love You and ever to grow progressively in that desire. Oh object of all my desires, increase in me the desire to love You, which You have given me. Increase it so much and make it so burning and strong that I may henceforth glow incessantly with the desire of Thy love.

5. Oh Jesus, worthy of all love, crown of all desire, ignite in my soul a thirst so ardent, and a hunger so extreme for your most Holy Love, that I would consider it a continual martyrdom to not love you enough. Grant that nothing in this world could afflict me more than to love you too meagerly.*

6. Oh Good Jesus! Who is there who would not wish to love You? Who would not desire to love ever more and more such lovable goodness? My God, my life and my all, I cannot be content to simply tell You that I desire to love You as perfectly as possible. I desire it so much that, if it were possible, I would will my whole spirit to be transformed into wishing, my whole soul into desire, my heart into yearning, my life into longing.

7. Oh King of my heart, take pity on my misery. You know that I want to love You. But alas! You see how much there is in me that goes against Your love. You see the innumerable multitude of my sins, my self-will, my self-love, my pride and all the other vices and imperfections which keep me from loving You perfectly. I detest and abhor all these defects which so obstruct my desire to love You! What must I do to destroy them? I stand ready to do and suffer all that pleases You for that end. Exert the strength of Your powerful arm to exterminate in my soul all the enemies of Your love.

---

* Elevation #5 was later used by Venerable Amelie Fristel (foundress of the Congregation of the Holy Hearts of Jesus and Mary) as her daily morning offering.

8. Oh Jesus, everything in You is love, and all love for me. And although I ought to be all love for You, there is in me nothing of myself, whether in body or in soul, that is not opposed to Your love. Oh, what pain! Oh, what anguish! How can I tolerate my own self? Where are You, divine love? Where is Your power? Where the force of Your mighty arm? Oh consuming and devouring fire, where are Your heavenly flames? Why do You not totally annihilate this wicked and sinful life of mine and establish Your life, divine and holy ?

9. Oh all-powerful love, I surrender myself entirely to Your holy might. Come, I beseech You, into my soul, there to destroy all that displeases You and to establish Your heavenly kingdom. If suffering is all that is required to effect this change, I offer myself with my whole heart to You that I may suffer all the martyrdom and torments that ever have been and ever shall be suffered in the world. Spare me not, love! Nothing matters except that I be set free from all that displeases my Savior and of all attachments that keep me from loving Him. I long to love my Jesus and I will to love Him perfectly, no matter what the cost, no matter what the sacrifice.

10. Oh God of love, You are all lovable, all loving, all love and all love for me. Why am I not also all love for You? Why are not heaven and earth transformed into a pure flame of love for You?

11. My sweet love, who shall henceforth prevent me from loving You, now that I realize Your immense goodness? Shall my body? I will grind it to dust first! Shall my past sins? Oh Jesus, I plunge them deep into the sea of Your Precious Blood. Take my body and my soul and make me suffer all that pleases You, to purge them utterly, so that they may no longer prevent me from loving You. Shall the world, or creatures stop me? No. With all my might I renounce all affections of sense and all created things. I consecrate my whole heart and all my affections to Jesus, my Creator and my God. And as for you, oh world, excommunicated from Jesus, since He and His disciples are not of this world, and since He said that He prayed not for the world, know once and for all that I give you up forever. I fly from you as from an excommunicate. It is my will to consider you as an antichrist, the enemy of my Lord Jesus Christ. I will set no more store by your praises and censures, your pleasures and ambitions, or by all that you most highly value and cherish than I would by a dream or a puff of smoke that vanishes away. I will hold in abhorrence your spirit, your code of behavior, your opinions and your accursed maxims. Finally, I will hate and persecute your malice just as much as you hate and persecute the goodness of my Lord Jesus Christ.

Farewell then, world, and once again farewell to all that is not God. Jesus shall henceforth be my world, my fame, my fortune, my delight and my all. I no longer desire to see anything but Jesus Christ. Eyes, inoculate yourself against all else, for He alone is a worthy object of vision. I no longer want to please anyone but Jesus. I no longer want to have any love or affection save for Him. I no longer want to rejoice except in His love and in performing His most amiable will. Nor do I any longer wish to grieve except for what offends Him and is contrary to His divine love. Oh love! Oh love! Let me love or let me die: nay, rather let me both love and die! Die to all that is not Jesus, and then love Him alone to perfection.

Elevations of the Heart Toward God

12. Oh King of my love, You have placed me on earth only that I may love You. Oh, how noble, how holy and how lofty is the end for which You have created me! Oh what a favor, oh my heart! What an honor was given you when you were created for the same purpose as the God who made you, and to employ yourself in the same divine activity which is His ceaseless concern! This great God exists only to contemplate and love Himself eternally and continually. My soul is created only to love the God who made it and to be forever employed in loving and blessing Him. May He be forever loved and blessed, the King of all hearts, who has given to me a heart capable of loving Him!

God of my heart, since You have created me only to love You, do not allow me to live except in love of You, ever growing in Your love. Let me love or let me die! Give me more life, my God, only that I may love You more. Better a thousand deaths than the loss of Your love.

13. Oh divine love, be the life of my life, soul of my soul, heart of my heart. Let me live no more unless it be in You and by You. Let me subsist no more unless it be by You and for You.

14. Oh sole object of my heart, You alone are worthy to be loved. All that is not You is mere nothingness and deserves not even one passing glance. It is You alone that I desire, You alone that I seek, You alone I long to love. You are my all; the rest is nothing to me now and I no longer want to regard anything or love anything, save You in all things.

Oh dearest Jesus, You are my greatest friend; indeed You are my one and only friend. To me You are Father, Brother, Spouse and Head. You are all mine. I desire to be all Yours forever.

15. Oh Jesus, who alone are worthy to be loved, who alone does love the Eternal Father, and who alone is loved in return by Him and by all the elect who love in heaven, grant that I may love You above all things, alone in all things, and that if I love any created thing, I may love it only in You and for You.

16. Oh only love of my heart! Oh sole object of my love! Nothing in heaven or on earth is worthy of love except You. When, therefore, shall it be ordained that men will see nothing and love nothing in heaven and on earth except You?

17. Oh Jesus, oh my one and only love, detach me altogether from myself and from all things. Draw me inescapably close to You. Possess me so fully and so absolutely that nothing but You may ever retain any part of my mind or my heart.

18. Oh Dearest Jesus! How lovable You are, and yet how little loved! The world thinks not of You, nor of loving You. it thinks only of offending You and of persecuting those who desire to love You. Let me then think of Your love instead of the world and concentrate all my thoughts on loving You! Grant that I may love You as much as the world ought to love You.

19. Oh Eternal Son of the Eternal Father, You are all lovable, all loving, and all love. From all eternity You began, without beginning. to love me forever. If I had existed from all eternity, I should have been bound to love You always. As I have only existed in time I should at least have loved You from the first moment I obtained the use of reason. Alas! I have begun to love You late indeed, nor do I even dare to say that I have even now begun to love You as I should. Oh Eternal God, You have never passed a moment without loving me, through all the extent of Your eternity, and yet I hardly know if I have ever spent a single moment of my life in loving You as I ought. On the contrary, I know only too well that I have never spent a day without offending You. What pain, what heartbreak for my soul, oh Lord; I can not tolerate myself when I think of this. Break with grief, oh my heart. Dissolve into tears, oh eyes! Why am I not dissolved into a sea of tears of penance and of blood, to lament and wipe out my prodigious ingratitude towards such great kindness! Oh love, no more offenses, no more sin, no more infidelity, no longer anything but love!

20. Oh eternal love, You are loved from all eternity by the Eternal Father and by the Holy Spirit. Boundless is my joy at this; I unite myself with this love, and I lose myself in the ceaseless love of the Father and the Holy Spirit for You from all eternity.

21. Oh everlasting beauty! Oh eternal goodness! If I had an eternity on earth, I should be bound to employ it all in Your love. How great, then, is my obligation to use what little life and time remain for me to love You! Oh dearest Lord, I consecrate it all to Your holy love. Grant that I may no longer live unless it be to love You, and that no moment of my life may pass without being employed in Your divine love! But above all, grant me to love You for all eternity. Whatever happens, I unite myself now with all the love that shall be Yours throughout eternity.

Oh eternity of love! My dearest Jesus, consume me with your divine Fire; dismember me, reduce me to dust and make me suffer every thing You may please in this world, provided only that I may love You eternally.

22. Oh King of Ages, You have bought, at the price of Your blood, every minute of my time and of my life so that I might use them in loving You. Too much, too much, alas, have I wasted on self-love, on love of the world and on attachment to created things. Too much time have I lost, time that has cost You so dearly, which ought to be so precious to me, since it could be employed in such great and important work as the infinite concerns of Your divine love. It is indeed time, oh Jesus, high time, that I begin seriously to practice the holy exercise of Your sacred love. Let me have no more days and hours, unless they are to love You. Let me so dispose my life that there may remain for me in all the world only myself and You. May I have nothing to do but think of You and converse with You, heart to heart, spirit to spirit. And may nothing, of all the things that happen in the world, touch me or pertain to me, save only the one care and the one desire to love You. Oh Jesus, increase in me this desire, and make it become so burning and so urgent that it may grow from a simple desire, into continual longing. May I aspire to You incessantly; may I tend towards You perpetually; may I yearn for You night and day without ceasing. Oh Sweetest Jesus, only love of my desires, when will the time come when I shall be utterly transformed into a pure flame of love for You?

23. Oh immense love, God of the Universe, You fill heaven and earth; You are everywhere and in all things. Everywhere You infinitely love the Father and the Holy Spirit, and are infinitely loved by Them. So, too, You love me infinitely in all places and in all things. Let me love You also in all places and all things, and let me love all things in You and for You. To that end, I unite myself to Your divine immensity, and in its fathomless power, I direct my mind and my will everywhere and into all places in the world. There, in all the power and immensity of Your spirit and Your love, I love You, glorify You and adore You infinitely. I also unite myself to the all-embracing love of Your Father and Your Holy Spirit for You, manifested everywhere and in all things that are in heaven, on earth and even in hell.

24. Oh infinite goodness, an infinite love would be necessary to love You as You deserve. What joy for my soul, what satisfaction for my heart, to know that You are so good, so perfect, and so lovable, even if all creatures on earth and in heaven were to exert all their strength, throughout eternity, they would never be able to love You enough. There is none but Yourself, together with the Father and the Holy Spirit, capable of loving You worthily.

25. Oh infinite goodness, if I had every single heart and the total capacity for love possessed by all men and angels, I should be bound to exert them all in the love of Him who is infinitely lovable, and directs all the sources of His wisdom, power and goodness to loving me and working so many wonders for my love. How great, then, is my obligation to exert my little strength in loving His goodness! Henceforth, oh my dear Jesus, I desire to pour forth all the powers of my body and soul in loving You. But that is not enough. I desire also to gather unto myself all the might of heaven and earth, which belong to me by Your gift of yourself, and exert them all in loving You. I desire to employ likewise all the powers of Your divinity and humanity, which are also mine, since You have Yourself given all of Yourself to me.

I love You, then, oh Jesus, I love You with all my might, with all the strength of my body and my soul, all the capacity of every creature in heaven and on earth, and all the powers of Your divinity and humanity.

26. But what am I saying, oh my God? I am not worthy to love You. To You alone belongs so holy and divine a function. Therefore I annihilate myself at Your feet, plunging into the deepest abyss of my nothingness. I give myself all to You. Destroy me Yourself by the power of that most mighty love, which reduced You even to the level of our nothingness, and establish in me Yourself, so that You may be loved in me with a love worthy of Yourself. Let me love You, henceforth, no longer by myself nor by the powers of my own mind and my own love, but by You and by Your mighty spirit and Your flaming love.

27. Oh most lovable Jesus, You assure us in Holy Scripture that the Father loves us even as He loves You, that is, with the same affection and the same love with which He loves You. You then command us to love You as You love the Heavenly Father and to remain ever in Your love, just as You always dwell in the love of the Father. But, Lord, You know my powerlessness to love You by myself. Grant me the grace to perform what You command of me; then command me as You wish. Destroy my own heart and my self-love. Implant within me Your Heart and Your love, so that I may henceforth love You as You love the Father and as the Father loves You. May I always remain in Your love, as You remain always in the love of Your Father; and may I do everything by the power and under the guidance of that love. Yes, my Jesus, it is in that eternal, infinite and immense love of the Father for You, and of You for the Father for all eternity, that I desire to love You from now on, consecrating to that love my every thought, word and deed for You. It is Your infinite love, Your immense Heart all filled with treasures of sublime love, that I offer to You as my own heart and love, since You gave it to me in giving me Yourself, together with the beloved heart of Your peerless Mother, the most lovable, the most loved, and the most loving of all human hearts. To these I add the hearts of all the saints and holy persons in heaven and on earth, and I offer them as my own, since Your holy apostle, St. Paul, teaches us that the Almighty Father, in giving You to us, gave us all things together with You (Rom. 8:32).

28. Oh Jesus, You are purity itself and You love me with an exceedingly pure love. I desire also to love You with the purest love possible. Hence, I wish to love You in Yourself, in Your own love; I desire to love nothing but You for Yourself alone, and solely for Your good pleasure. I love You, oh my dearest Jesus, I love You with that exceeding pure love You have for Yourself. I love you also in the most pure love of the Eternal Father, the Holy Spirit, Your most pure Mother, Your angels and Your saints. Oh Father of Jesus, angels of Jesus and His saints, all you creatures, come to my aid. Help me to love your Creator and mine. Come, let us love Him, our most lovable Lord, let us employ and expend all our being and all our powers in loving Him who created us only that we might love Him.

29. Oh dearest Friend of my heart and dearest Heart of my love! How desolate it is, and how much to be lamented with tears of blood, to see You loved so little even by those who claim to love You.

And this is strange because there is no one so worthy of love as You; yet it seems there is nothing in the world less loved than You. There are many souls who love the thought of heaven and the sweetness of Your grace and the consolations of Your love, but out of a thousand good men scarcely one will be found to love You purely for love of Yourself alone. Oh most pure love, my dearest Savior, You alone do I seek, You alone do I desire, You alone do I love. I desire to love You not for my own interest and satisfaction, not because it is sweet and full of consolation, but because You are most worthy to be loved for Yourself alone.

30. When shall I love You so purely that I shall be able to say with truth: My Jesus is my all and everything else to me is nothing. He alone suffices for me, and I desire no other. I desire Him not for myself but for His own goodness. The joys of Paradise, the consolation of heavenly love, are not my aim. I seek the Lord of Paradise and the divine Author of all consolations. And even if He were never to favor me with any consolations or reward (which would not be possible to His goodness), yet should I wish to love Him always because He is most worthy of love. I desire no other reward than to have the power to love Him for His own sake alone.

Oh good Jesus, implant these loving dispositions in my heart and in the hearts of all mankind especially those to whom You know I am indebted and eager to remember in my prayers. Oh King of all hearts, behold I offer to You each poor human heart You have created to love You, desiring now only to breathe Your love. Destroy in those chosen hearts all that is contrary to Your sacred affection; fill them with Your divine love. Oh dearest Savior, draw them to Yourself; unite them to Your Sacred Heart; engulf them in Your love and number them among the blessed of whom it is said: "Their hearts shall live for ever and ever" (Ps. 21:27), that is, they shall live with the life of divine love, in order to love forever the God of love and of life! How blessed are the hearts consecrated for all eternity to adore, praise and love the most adorable and exceedingly lovable Heart of Jesus! Blessed be He who has created these cherished hearts that He might be glorified and loved by them forever!

31. Oh God of my life and of my heart, You love me constantly. You employ all Your powers and all creation in heaven and on earth, to testify to me of Your love. I learn from one of Your dearest saints: "Heaven and earth and all creation never cease to tell me that I should love the Lord my God" (St. Augustine, *Manuale*, c.24). Everything that I hear, everything I see, taste, touch and smell, everything that can be known or desired by my memory, understanding and will, all things visible and invisible that are contained in the order of nature, grace and glory, all the temporal and eternal graces I have received from You, all the angels and saints, all the encouraging examples they have given me by their virtues and their holy lives, all the wonders You have worked on behalf of Your most holy Mother, all the perfections inherent in the essence of Your Divine Person, all the mysteries of Your divinity and humanity, all Your divine attributes and virtues, all Your thoughts, words, deeds and sufferings, every step You took on earth, every drop of Your Precious Blood, all the wounds of Your sacred body, in a word, all things that are or ever were, in created or uncreated being, in time and in eternity, constitute so many tongues by which You continually proclaim to me Your goodness and Your love. All these things incessantly testify that You love me and urge me to love You in return. All are so many voices by which You say constantly to me: "I love you, I love you! Love Me for I have loved you first. Love the Lord your God with your whole heart and your whole soul and your whole strength." Finally, all these things are so many preachers, so many voices crying out to me without ceasing: "Love, love for Jesus, who is all love for you, who employs all that He is, all that He has, all that He knows, all that He does and all that depends on Him, in heaven and on earth, to make you realize the love He bears you, and to win your heart and entice you to love Him."

My Lord and my God, how surpassingly great is Your bounty and how wonderful Your love for me! You love, desire and seek me with intensity and fervor, as if I were of great concern to You, as if I were indeed truly necessary to You. You desire to possess me and fear to lose me as if I were a precious treasure. You pursue my friendship with as much insistence as if Your happiness depended upon it. Would there be anything more You could do for me, oh Lord, even if Your whole happiness and glory did depend upon my love? Oh profound kindness, I lose myself in Your fathomless depths.

Oh priceless kindness, how can it be You are so little valued, so little loved, and so much offended and persecuted by those whom You love so? Oh hearts of men, how hardened you must be not to be softened by so many persuasive and loving voices! How frozen, not to be melted by so many sacred fires and flames! How can I resist so many powerful attractions of Your infinite kindness? What do You desire or expect of me, oh my Savior, except that I reply to You with St. Peter, the Prince of the apostles: "I love You, I love You" (John 21:15-17).

But instead of replying to You in this way, I have cried out against You with the cruel Jews, by the voice of my sins: "Take Him away, take Him away. Crucify Him!" (John 19:15). Oh what anguish and heart rending sorrow! All my sins, my ingratitude, my perverse inclinations, my self-love, my self-will, my pride, all my other vices, all my evil thoughts, words and actions, all the misuse of my bodily senses, of spiritual faculties, all are so many voices worthy of hell that clamor against You unceasingly with the Jews: Take Him away, take Him away. Crucify Him. Oh detestable traitor! Is this how you love Him who is all love for you? Is this your answer to Him who calls you with such sweet persuasion to His love? Is this how you repay His unbounded kindness for all the blessings you have received from Him? Forgive me, oh most generous Lord, I beseech You, forgive me. May all Your kindness and mercies (if I be permitted to say it thus) ask forgiveness for me. May Your holy Mother, with all the angels and saints, cast themselves down at Your feet to win this pardon from Your clemency. May all the creatures by which You cry out to me, "I love you," be so many suppliants on my behalf before the throne of Your kindness, crying with all the humility, repentance and contrition that ever was or ever shall be: "Forgive, forgive, have mercy on this poor sinner!"

Oh most merciful Savior, may it please You to accept and approve by Your great mercy the promises I am about to make for the future. Oh my most lovable Jesus, since You constantly love me, and since You employ all that is within and without Yourself in loving me, I, too, desire to be ever focused on loving You, employing all that is within and without me in Your holy love. And even if, to imagine the impossible, I were to be in no way under obligation to love You, I should, nevertheless, desire to love You with my whole heart and all my strength.

To that end, if it pleases You, I desire to dedicate all my thoughts, words and deeds, all the functions and senses of my body and faculties of my soul, my every breath and heartbeat, every pulse of my veins, every instant of my life, all things that have been, are, and shall be in me, even my sins, so far as it is possible, to Your wisdom, which well knows how to make all things cooperate for the good of those who love You. I desire that all these things may turn into so many voices, by which I may continue ceaselessly and eternally telling You, with all the love in heaven and on earth: "I love You, I love You, yes, my Lord Jesus, I love You." And if any element of my soul or part of my body says the contrary, I desire that it may be ground into powder and cast to the winds.

32. I also desire that all things that ever were, are and shall be in the orders of nature, grace and glory, in heaven or on earth and even in hell, may be as many voices proclaiming without ceasing forever, on my behalf: "I love You, I love You, Lord Jesus." This is the spiritual use I am bound and freely desire to make of all things, in so far as they belong to me and have been given to me by You to employ in Your love.

33. I also desire further, oh my Jesus, that all the powers and perfections of Your divinity and humanity, all Your states, mysteries, attributes, virtues, thoughts, words, acts and sufferings, all Your sacred wounds, every drop of Your precious blood, every moment of Your eternity (if such an expression be permissible), all things that are or ever existed in Your body, soul and divinity, may be so many voices proclaiming to You forever for me: "I love You, oh most loving Jesus; I love You, oh infinite goodness; I love You, with my whole heart, with my whole soul, and all my might. I desire to love You ever more and more."

Finally, my Savior, I desire, if it pleases You, that there may no, longer be anything in existence, in my body or in my soul, in my life and my eternity, which is not transformed into love for You.

In order to implement my desires and wishes effectively, I desire and will all this, not with my human and natural will, which is too weak and unworthy to he employed in willing such great and holy things, but with Your divine will, oh Jesus, which is all powerful and belongs to me, since You are all mine.

Oh my Lord, if my powers were as great as my desires, I should indeed make everything achieve its perfect fulfillment for Your glory and love. But it is for me to desire and for You to carry out. You can do all things, and you do the will of those that fear You. Grant, then, these my cherished and deepest desires, oh most beloved Jesus. I beg this of You by all that You are, by Your infinite goodness and mercy, by everything You love, and by all who love You in heaven and on earth for Your most pure love and satisfaction. Your love is mine and since I will what I have said in the power of Your divine will, my confidence is firm that, in Your infinite goodness, all these things shall be effected as Your eternal wisdom deems most fitting to the glory of Your divine greatness.

34. Good Jesus, when will the time come when there will no longer remain anything in me to prevent me from loving you? Too well I know that this shall never be on earth, but only in heaven. Oh beautiful heaven! How you appeal to my desires! Oh blessed city where Jesus is perfectly loved and His glorious love fully reigns, where no hearts dwell that are not completely transformed in this divine love! Oh earth, oh world, oh body, dark prison of my soul, how unbearable you are! Wretch that I am, who shall deliver me from the body of this death? Do I still have long to remain in this miserable exile, in this strange land, in this place of sin and accursedness? Will not that day soon come, that desirable hour for which I have so often longed, in which I shall begin to love most perfectly my most lovable Lord?

My dearest Jesus, shall I then never love You as I desire? God of mercy, will You not take pity upon my sorrow? Will You refuse to hear my supplication? Will You not grant what I implore with such pitiful cries? Oh my Lord, to You do I cry, it is You whom I desire, for You I long. Well You know that I desire nothing on heaven or earth, in life or in death, except Your pure love.

Mother of Christ, angels and saints of Christ and all His creatures, take pity on my sorrow; speak on my behalf to the Beloved of my soul; tell Him that I pine away with love for Him. Tell Him that I desire nothing in time or eternity but His pure love; I desire neither heaven, nor the glory of heaven, nor the great joys of paradise, nor the delights of His grace, but only His most pure love. Tell Him that I can no longer live without that pure love. I implore Him to make haste, to fulfill in me the designs and work of His grace and to consume me utterly in His divine love, in order to take me soon into His eternal kingdom. "Amen. Come, Lord Jesus" (Rev 22:20). Come, my life and my light, come, my love, my all, come unto me and eradicate everything that works against Your love. Come to me to transform me wholly into love for You. Come to draw me to You, and to establish me soon in that abode of love where true and perfect love reigns, where all is love, pure and continual, changeless and everlasting. Come, oh dearest Jesus, the only love of my heart.

Acts of Love for Jesus, Prisoner in the Sacred Womb of His Most Blessed Mother

Oh Jesus, my love, I behold You as a prisoner in the most pure womb of Your Blessed Mother, but more imprisoned in the sacred bonds of Your divine love. Let me love You, oh good Jesus, in the infinite love that binds You and make me, with You, a prisoner of divine love.

Oh Love that holds Jesus captive in Mary and Mary in Jesus, take my heart, my mind, my thoughts, desires and affections prisoner and establish Jesus in me, in order that I may be completely filled with Him, and that He may live and reign perfectly in me.

Oh Jesus, my sweet love, I love You with all the love with which You were loved during Your nine months' imprisonment, by Your Eternal Father, Your Holy Spirit, Your Blessed Mother, St. Joseph, St. Gabriel, and all the angels and saints who took some special part in this mystery of love.

Oh abyss of love, when I behold You in the sacred womb of Your most holy Mother, I see You as it were divinely lost and submerged in the ocean of Your divine love. Let me lose myself, and be immersed with You in this same love!

Acts of Love in Honor of the Birth and Holy Childhood of Jesus

Oh Jesus, You are infinite love in all the moments, states and mysteries of Your life, but, above all, You are pure love and sweetness at the moment of Your birth and during Your most Holy Childhood. Let me love You at this precious moment, in this hidden state. May heaven and earth join with me and may the whole world be transformed into love for its Creator and God, who is completely transformed into gentleness and love for the world.

Oh most amiable Child, You are born by love, in love and for love. At the moment of Your birth, You love Your Eternal Father more than all angels and men together could do in all eternity. So, too, the Heavenly Father loves You more at this moment than He ever did or will love all men and angels together.

Oh Jesus, I offer You all the love concentrated on You at birth by Your Eternal Father, by Your Holy Spirit, Your Blessed Mother, St. Joseph, St. Gabriel and all the angels and saints who participated so intimately in this most lovable mystery.

Oh Love of Jesus, that triumphs over Him in all His mysteries, but particularly in His sublime childhood and the consummation of His cross, oh Love that in these two mysteries, transforms His omnipotence into helplessness, His plenitude into poverty, His sovereignty into dependence, His eternal wisdom into infancy, His joy and bliss into sufferings, and His life into death, conquer my self-love, my own will and my passions. Put me in a state of powerlessness, indigence, dependence, holy and divine childhood, and death to the world and to myself. Thus I may adore and glorify the powerlessness, the dependence, childhood and death to which you reduced my Jesus in the mysteries of His nativity and of His cross.

Conclusion

These 34 acts of divine love, along with those upon the nativity and childhood of Jesus will suffice to show you how to make similar acts in honor of the other mysteries of the life of our most lovable Jesus

I have suggested these little practices to point out the way you must follow in order to walk ever before God and live in the spirit of Jesus. This spirit will inspire many other methods in your heart if you make a point of giving yourself to our Blessed Lord at the beginning of everything you do. For I beg you to note carefully that the one essential practice, the secret of secrets, the devotion of devotions, is to be attached to no one practice or exercise of devotion in particular, but to take care, in all your exercises and activities, to surrender yourself to the holy spirit of Jesus, with humility, confidence and detachment from all things.

When you are thus free from attachment to your own way of looking at things, or to your own devotions and tastes, He will have complete power and freedom to act in you according to His holy will. He will arouse in your soul whatever dispositions and devout sentiments He desires, and lead you by whatever paths He may choose. After you have given yourself to Him, you should progress and be faithful in cultivating the good sentiments and dispositions He will arouse in you, and in following His suggestions, inspirations, and guidance. If He inspires you to make use of the above exercises, and if they prove to be a source of grace and blessings to you, well and good! If He attracts you to other more perfect ways, or methods in which you find more grace and devotion, follow His attractions with simplicity and humility.

ADDENDA

A Note on the Translator

In late 1941, the young **Thomas Merton** left his existence in the world to seek the freedom of cloistered life.

At the Trappist Abbey of Our Lady of Gethsemani novices were immersed in work and silence for two years before beginning serious study. Because of his mastery of language, one assignment given to the young frater (as novices were then called) was to translate certain spiritual classics from French. During Lent of 1943, he was given *The Life and Kingdom of Jesus* by St. John Eudes with an aggressive deadline for completion. His early autobiography describes the harrowing work:

Thomas Merton

> "After the Conventual Mass, I would get out book and pencil and papers and go to work at one of the long tables in the novitiate scriptorium, filling the yellow sheets as fast as I could, while another novice took them and typed them as soon as they were finished."[1]

Despite this pressure from the publisher, the project was completed on time. Merton's superior called the finished product "the best translation of any of the works of St. John Eudes that he had seen."[2] Archbishop Fulton Sheen agreed in his introduction to this edition of *The Kingdom*, exulting that the spiritual treatise was "now so ably translated into English."[3]

This took place years before Merton's "Seven Storey Mountain" was released to the public, so his name did not yet hold great value to the publishers. In the spirit of humility and silence, Merton accepted for his translation to be attributed simply to "A Trappist Father in The Abbey of Our Lady of Gethsemani."[4]

---

1 Thomas Merton, *The Seven Storey Mountain* (New York: Harcourt, Brace & Company, 1948), 401.
2 Benjamin Clark, OCSO, "Thomas Merton's Gethsemani: Part 1, the Novitiate Years," *The Merton Annual, vol. 4* (1991): 250.
3 Fulton J Sheen, Introduction to *The Life and Kingdom of Jesus in Christian Souls,* by

St. John Eudes (New York: PJ Kennedy & Sons, 1946), xix.

4   The attribution to a "Trappist *father*" is curious given that Merton would not be ordained until 1949. However, there is no doubt that the work is his. Fr. Benjamin Clark OCSO was the "other novice" referred to in the Seven Storey Mountain. Fr. Clark recalls:
> "I remember one such assignment which Merton records (SSM, p. 401). Gethsemani had entered a contract to translate the work of St. John Eudes for the publication of a new edition. Several of the monks had been assigned volumes to translate, and Merton was given The Kingdom of Jesus in Christian Souls. The publishers had allowed only a short time for the work to be completed and so I was assigned to help Merton meet the deadline. I typed the finished copy in triplicate as Merton dashed off the original on sheets of yellow paper." "Thomas Merton's Gethsemani," p. 249.

About St. John Eudes

Born in France on November 14, 1601, St. John Eudes' life spanned the "Great Century." The Age of Discovery had revolutionized technology and exploration; the Council of Trent initiated a much-needed reform in the Church; among the common people, it was the dawn of a golden age of sanctity and mystic fervor.

His Spiritual Heritage

No fewer than seven Doctors of the Church had lived in the previous century. Great reformers like St. Francis de Sales, St. Teresa of Avila, and St. John of the Cross had left an indelible mark on the Catholic faith. Their influence was still fresh as St. John Eudes came onto the scene.

He was educated by the Jesuits in rural Normandy. He was ordained into the Oratory of Jesus and Mary, a society of priests which had just been founded on the model of St. Philip Neri's Oratory in Rome. The founder was Cardinal Pierre de Bérulle, a man renowned for his holiness and named "the apostle of the Incarnate Word" by Pope Urban VII. Rounding out St. John Eudes' heritage is the influence of the Discalced Carmelites. His spiritual director, Cardinal Bérulle himself, had brought sisters from St. Teresa of Avila's convent to help found the Carmel in France. John Eudes would later become spiritual director to a Carmelite convent himself. Their cloister prayed constantly for his missionary activity.

His Life of Ministry

As an avid participant in a wave of re-evangelization in France, St. John Eudes' principal apostolate was preaching parish missions. Spending anywhere from 4 to 20 weeks in each parish, he preached over 120 missions across his lifetime, always with a team of confessors providing the sacrament around the clock, and catechists meeting daily with small groups of parishioners.

Early in his priesthood, an outbreak of plague hit St. John Eudes' native region and he rushed to provide sacraments to the dying. The risk of contagion was so great no one else dared to approach the victims. In order to protect his Oratorian brothers from contagion, St. John Eudes took up residence in a large empty cider barrel outside of the city walls until the plague had ended.

His Foundations

During his missions he heard countless confessions himself, including those from women forced into prostitution. Realizing that they needed intense healing and support, he began to found "Houses of Refuge" to help them get off the street and begin a new life. In 1641 he founded the Sisters of Our Lady of Charity of the Refuge to continue this work. They would live with the penitent women and provide them with constant support. Today, these sisters are known as the Good Shepherd Sisters, inspired by their fourth vow of zeal to go out seeking the "lost sheep."

Occasionally, St. John Eudes would return to the site of a previous mission. To his dismay, he found that the fruits of the mission were consistently fading for lack of support. The crucial piece in need of change was the priesthood. At that time, the only way to be trained as a priest was through apprenticeship. The result of this training was so horribly inconsistent that the term "hocus pocus" was invented during this time to describe the corrupted Latin used by poorly trained priests during the consecration at mass. In 1643 he left the Oratory and founded the Congregation of Jesus and Mary to found a seminary. Seminary training was a radical brand-new concept which had just been proposed by the Council of Trent.

His Mark on the Church

At a mission in 1648 St. John Eudes authored the first mass in history in honor of the Heart of Mary. In 1652 he built the first church under the Immaculate Heart's patronage: the chapel of his seminary in Coutances, France. During the process of his canonization, Pope St. Pius X named St. John Eudes "the father, doctor, and apostle of liturgical devotion to the hearts of Jesus and Mary." The Heart of Jesus because he created the first Feast of the Sacred Heart in 1672, just one year before St. Margaret Mary Alacoque had her first apparition of the Sacred Heart.

Although his Marian devotion was intense from a tender age, the primary inspiration for this feast came from St. John Eudes' theology of baptism. From the beginning of his missionary career he taught that Jesus continues His Incarnation in the life of each baptized Christian. As we give ourselves to Christ, our hands become His hands, our heart is transformed into His heart. Mary is the ultimate exemplar of this. She gave her heart to God so completely that she and Jesus have just one heart between them. Thus, whoever sees Mary, sees Jesus, and honoring the heart of Mary is never separate from honoring the heart of Jesus.

Doctor of the Church?

At the time of this writing, Bishops the world over have requested that the Vatican proclaim St. John Eudes as a Doctor of the Church. This would recognize his unique contribution to our understanding of the Gospel, and his exemplary holiness of life which stands out even among saints. For more information on the progress of this cause, on his writings or spirituality, or to sign up for our e-newsletter updates, contact spirituality@eudistsusa.org.

About the Eudist Family

During his lifetime, St. John Eudes' missionary activity had three major areas of focus.
- For priests, he provided formation, education, and the spiritual support which is crucial for their role in God's plan of salvation.
- For prostitutes and others on the margins of society, he gave them a home and bound their wounds, like the Good Shepherd with his lost sheep.
- For the laity, he preached the dignity of their baptism and their responsibility to be the hands and feet of God, to continue the Incarnation.

In everything he did, he burned with the desire to be a living example of the love and mercy of God.

These are the "family values" which continue to inspire those who continue his work. To paraphrase St. Paul, John Eudes planted seeds, which others watered through the institutions he founded, and God gave the growth. Today, the family tree continues to bear fruit:

The *Congregation of Jesus and Mary* (CJM), also known as The Eudists, continues the effort to form and care for priests and other leaders within the Church. St. John Eudes called this the mission of "teaching the teachers, shepherding the shepherds, and enlightening those who are the light of the world." Continuing his efforts as a missionary preacher, Eudist priests and brothers "audaciously seek to open up new avenues for evangelization," through television, radio, and new media.

The *Religious of the Good Shepherd* (RGS) continue outreach to women in difficult situations, providing them with a deeply needed place of refuge and healing while they seek a new life. St. Mary Euphrasia drastically expanded the reach of this mission which now operates in over 70 countries worldwide. A true heiress of St. John Eudes, St. Mary Euphrasia exhorted her sisters: "We must go after the lost sheep with no other rest than the cross, no other consolation than work, and no other thirst than for justice."

In every seminary and House of Refuge founded by St. John Eudes, he also established a *Confraternity of the Holy Heart of Jesus and Mary* for the laity, now known as the Eudist Associates. The mission he gave them was twofold: First, "To glorify the divine Hearts of Jesus and Mary... working to make them live and reign in their own heart through diligent imitation of their virtues." Second, "To work for the salvation of souls... by practicing, according to their abilities, works of charity and mercy and by attaining numerous graces through prayer for the clergy and other apostolic laborers."

The *Little Sisters of the Poor* were an outgrowth of this confraternity. St. Jeanne Jugan was formed as a consecrated woman within the Eudist Family. She discovered the great need for love and mercy among the poor and elderly and the mission took on a life of its own. She passed on to them the Eudist intuition that the poor are not simply recipients of charity, they provide an encounter with Charity Himself: "My little ones, never forget that the poor are Our Lord... In serving the aged, it is He Himself whom you are serving."

A more recent "sprout" on the tree was founded by Mother Antonia Brenner in Tijuana, Mexico. After raising her children in Beverly Hills and suffering through divorce, she followed God's call to become a live-in prison minister at the *La Mesa* penitentiary. The *Eudist Servants of the 11th Hour* was founded so that other women in the latter part of their lives could imitate her in "being love" to those most in need.

The example St. John Eudes set for living out the Gospel has inspired many more individuals and organizations throughout the world. For more information about the Eudist family, news on upcoming publications, or for ways to share in our mission, contact us at spirituality@eudistsusa.org.

34 Flames of Divine Love: Elevations of the Heart Towards God

For more from St. John Eudes, Eudist Press offers individual prayerbooks that shine a spotlight on different aspects of his spirituality. Each one is an excerpt from his classic bestseller: *The Life and the Kingdom of Jesus: A Treatise on Christian Perfection for Use by Clergy or Laity,* translated from French by Thomas Merton in The Abbey of Our Lady of Gethsémani and published by Kennedy & Sons in New York, 1946.

They can be found at https://www.eudistsusa.org/publications.

More by Eudist Press
- *A Heart on Fire: St. John Eudes, a Model for the New Evangelization*
- *Spiritual Itinerary for Today with St. John Eudes*
- *Eudist Lectionary: A St. John Eudes Reader*

Eudist Prayerbook Series
- Volume 1: *Heart of the Holy Family: A Manual of Prayer*
- Volume 2: *More than Just 50 Beads: Rosary Meditations for the Liturgical Year*
- Volume 3: *A Holy Week Every Week: Weekday Meditations*
- Volume 4: *34 Flames of Divine Love: Elevations of the Heart Towards God*
- Volume 5: *On the Threshold of Life: A Self-Directed Retreat to Celebrate your Birthday*
- Volume 6: *On the Threshold of Eternity: A Self-Directed Retreat to Prepare for a Happy Death*

Biography
- *St. John Eudes: An Artisan of Christian Renewal of the Seventeenth Century*
- *In All Things, the Will of God: St. John Eudes Through His Letters*

More by St. John Eudes
St. John Eudes' Selected Works
- *The Life and Kingdom of Jesus in Christian Souls*
- *The Sacred Heart of Jesus*
- *The Admirable Heart of Mary*
- *The Priest: His Dignity and Obligations*
- *Meditations*
- *Letters and Shorter Works*

Other Works
- *Man's Contract with God in Holy Baptism*
- *The Wondrous Childhood of the Mother of God*

www.ingramcontent.com/pod-product-compliance
Lightning Source LLC
Chambersburg PA
CBHW041756040426
42446CB00001B/52